Legends of the Ancient World: The Hanging Gardens of Babylon

By Charles River Editors

1912 sketch depicting the Hanging Gardens of Babylon

Introduction

A 16th-century colored engraving of the Hanging Gardens of Babylon by Dutch artist Martin Heemskerck, with the Tower of Babel in the background

The Hanging Gardens of Babylon

"There was also, beside the acropolis, the Hanging Garden, as it is called, which was built, not by Semiramis, but by a later Syrian king to please one of his concubines; for she, they say, being a Persian by race and longing for the meadows of her mountains, asked the king to imitate, through the artifice of a planted garden, the distinctive landscape of Persia." Diodorus Siculus

In antiquity, the Hanging Gardens, like the Great Pyramid of Giza, were considered both a technological marvel and an aesthetic masterpiece. Ancient historians believed that the Hanging Gardens were constructed around the 7th century B.C. after the second rise of Babylon, which would make them the second-oldest of the Seven Wonders of the Ancient World. Reputedly, they were created by the biblical Nebuchadnezzar II (the king who conquered Judea) to please his homesick wife, after the model of Egyptian pleasure gardens, but in 1993, British Assyriologist, Stephanie Dalley, proposed a theory that they were ordered built by the Assyrian King Sennacherib a century earlier for his giant palace at Nineveh, instead. She believed that the two sites were easily confused by ancient sources, resulting in the Gardens being incorrectly located in Babylon a century later.

Many ancient writers discussed the Hanging Gardens, including Strabo, Diodorus Siculus, and Quintus Curtius Rufus. In fact, Diodorus Siculus and Philo of Byzantium both described the mechanisms of the Gardens at length. According to their accounts, the Hanging Gardens were terraced and cultivated orchards that were built over a series of buildings made of glazed ceramic and perhaps watered by some kind of pulley or pump system of irrigation. Water was drawn from a reservoir through a network of reeds and bricks, held together by asphalt and cement, with lead used as a sealant. The Gardens were built on a citadel 80 feet high with walls 22 feet thick.

Despite the detailed descriptions, historians still question whether the Hanging Gardens ever actually existed. The sheer amount of water that would've been required, and the fact that they would've relied on technology that was supposedly invented 400 years down the line cast doubt upon their existence. Officially, the reason why it is not known whether the Hanging Gardens ever existed is because they were reported to have been destroyed by several earthquakes, the last of which left the Hanging Gardens completely ruined by the 2nd century B.C., around the time the Greek "tourists" were writing their pamphlets. Therefore, it is not known if any of the writers who described them ever truly saw the Hanging Gardens, and even as ancient Greeks and Romans of different centuries wrote about the Hanging Gardens and relied on previous ancient texts, Babylonian sources do not mention them. Neither do near-contemporaneous Greek sources like Herodotus.

Legends of the Ancient World: The Hanging Gardens of Babylon comprehensively covers the history and mystery of the famous wonder of the ancient world, looking at ancient descriptions of the Hanging Gardens and the questions modern academics are still trying to answer. Along with pictures and a bibliography, you will learn about the Hanging Gardens like you never have before, in no time at all.

Chapter 1: A Wonder of the Ancient World

The Hanging Gardens of Babylon were such a sight to behold that they featured prominently even among the very earliest lists of the seven wonders of the ancient world. The idea of listing the seven wonders of the world is one that developed in ancient Greece and remains popular in the imagination of the Western world today. The natural world is full of majesty and wonder that causes people to look on in astonishment and awe, but the ancient Greeks reserved their highest praise for monumental human achievements, works that, like the fabled Tower of Babel, would cause the gods to fear that humanity has learned to work together in such harmony that nothing will be impossible for them.

Although the Hanging Gardens and the company they kept are universally known today as the Seven Wonders of the Ancient World, the group of seven were not originally labeled as "wonders" (*thaumata* in Greek), but as "sights" (*theamata* in Greek) (Clayton and Price, 1988, 4). They were included in ancient Greek travel guides as the must-see destinations for affluent travelers who were curious to see the best of what the rest of the world had to offer. This conceptualization of such "sights" was typified by Herodotus, the 5th century B.C. Greek historian. In his life's work, the *Histories*, Herodotus speaks fondly of the city of Babylon and of Egypt and its pyramids, though it must be noted he did not make any specific mention of hanging gardens.

The Greeks had a high regard for tradition, antiquity and wealth, and it was abundantly clear that the Egyptian and Babylonian civilizations possessed each of these qualities. When Alexander the Great conquered the Persian armies and wrested control of their great empire for himself in the 4th century, there was a major emphasis on what united the eastern and western parts of his empire. It was during this Hellenistic period that the fascinating sights (*theamata*) became "wonders" (*thaumata*). It was no coincidence that the locations of the original seven wonders not only fell within the confines of Alexander's empire but also marked the vast expanse of it.

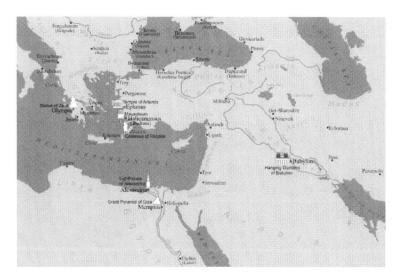

A map showing the locations of the Seven Wonders of the Ancient World

Callimachus of Cyrene wrote a work in the 3rd century B.C. entitled "A Collection of Wonders in Lands throughout the World." All that remains of this work is the name of it, but the title itself indicates Greek writers were compiling lists of remarkable human achievements. The most recently built "wonder" that made the canonical list of seven was the statue of Helios in Rhodes, which was completed during Callimachus's lifetime, though it is impossible to say whether such a recent work of craftsmanship made it into Callimachus' work.

Whatever the case, by the mid-2nd century B.C., the list of seven had become fixed. These seven were preserved in a poem written by Antipater of Sidon, which reads:

> "I have gazed on the walls of impregnable Babylon,
>
> along which chariots may race,
>
> and on the Zeus by the banks of the Alpheus,
>
> I have seen the Hanging Gardens
>
> and the Colossus of Helios,
>
> the great man-made mountains of the lofty pyramids,
>
> and the gigantic tomb of Maussollos.

But when I saw the sacred house of Artemis that towers to the clouds,

the others were placed in the shade,

for the sun himself has never looked upon its equal outside

Olympus." (Antipater, *Greek Anthology*, IX 58)

While the poet sets apart the temple of Artemis from the rest of the list, in many ways the Hanging Gardens stand out as a mystery within this list. There are no outstanding questions about the other wonders in terms of what they are, when they were constructed, or where they are located, yet the Hanging Gardens present anomalies in each of these areas. Ancient visitors who presumably would have or should have seen such a marvelous sight remain silent on the matter, and modern archeologists excavating the site fumble around in trying to identify any trace of such an agricultural feat among the city's remains. Assyriologists continue to search in vain for any firsthand or primary references to this wonder that clearly astounded generations of Greeks. But historians love these kinds of mysteries, which allow them to don their detective hats and try to come up with an explanation.

Chapter 2: Ancient Descriptions of the Hanging Gardens

Despite a lack of primary sources, there is certainly no lack of secondary sources, as the Hanging Gardens appear in a half a dozen or so ancient Greek sources. Moreover, while the descriptions differ in some minor details, they largely agree on the main points.

It is important to keep in mind that although they shared a great deal in common in terms of their writing system and their religion, the Assyrians and the Babylonians were two distinct cultural groups with distinctive empires in ancient Mesopotamia. They can be thought of as very similar to the Greek and Roman empires in terms of cultural proximity. They spoke different but closely related languages, they had similar pantheons (with different names for the same deities), and the geographic extent of their empires overlapped a great deal at their peaks. Various native Babylonians in the 4th and 3rd centuries B.C. set to writing histories of the Assyrian and Babylonian empires for consumption by Greek audiences, who appreciated ancient civilizations and religious rituals. Thus, most of the surviving sources referring to the Hanging Gardens came secondhand from Greek authors quoting works by these native authors.

It is worth reviewing the actual Greek sources that speak of the Hanging Gardens in chronological order, but even here, there's a problem in deciding upon the chronological order of these sources. For example, they could be aligned by the dates of the sources themselves, or they can be aligned by the dates of the primary sources referred to. This chapter is arranged by looking at the chronological order of the sources referred to by the Greek writers.

From 60-30 B.C., an ancient Greek historian named Diodorus Siculus wrote historical works, and he relied on a history of Alexander the Great written by Cleitarchus of Alexandria in the 4th century B.C. Relying on that source, Diodorus Siculus wrote about the Hanging Gardens:

> "There was also, beside the acropolis, the Hanging Garden, as it is called, which was built, not by Semiramis, but by a later Syrian king to please one of his concubines; for she, they say, being a Persian by race and longing for the meadows of her mountains, asked the king to imitate, through the artifice of a planted garden, the distinctive landscape of Persia. The park extended four plethra on each side, and since the approach to the garden sloped like a hillside and the several parts of the structure rose from one another tier on tier, the appearance of the whole resembled that of a theatre. When the ascending terraces had been built, there had been constructed beneath them galleries which carried the entire weight of the planted garden and rose little by little one above the other along the approach; and the uppermost gallery, which was fifty cubits high, bore the highest surface of the park, which was made level with the circuit wall of the battlements of the city. Furthermore, the walls, which had been constructed at great expense, were twenty-two feet thick, while the passageway between each two walls was ten feet wide. The roofs of the galleries were covered over with beams of stone sixteen foot long, inclusive of the overlap, and four feet wide. The roof above these beams had first a layer of reeds laid in great quantities of bitumen, over these two courses of baked brick bonded by cement, and as a third layer a covering of lead, to the end that the moisture from the soil might not penetrate beneath. On all this again the earth had been piled to a depth sufficient for the roots of the largest trees; and the ground, when leveled off, was thickly planted with trees of every kind that, by their great size or any other charm, could give pleasure to the beholder. And since the galleries, each projecting beyond another, all received the light, they contained many royal lodges of every description; and there was one gallery which contained openings leading from the topmost surface and machines for supplying the gardens with water, the machines raising the water in great abundance from the river, although no one outside could see it being done." (*Library*, 2.10)

Some interesting facts to note from this earliest source are that the queen for whom the garden was built is not named, aside from the specification that it was not Semiramis. This suggests that a lot of people in Diodorus' day were claiming Semiramis as the queen in question.

Furthermore, the reference to the Syrian king is actually an English translation issue. The Greek word syros was confusingly translated by scholars from an earlier generation as "Syrian". In fact, the word syros was a reference to Assyrian; Herodotus clarified the situation when he wrote, "The Greeks call these people Syrians, but others know them as Assyrians."

The emphasis in the description is in the mountain-like quality of the gardens. There is also reference to a water-raising device for irrigation, but no details appear on the specifics of such a device. The first known engineering device that could raise water from a source was the Archimedes Screw, named after the famous 3rd century genius from Syracuse. Archimedes, widely hailed as antiquity's greatest scientist, lived about 400 years after the Hanging Gardens were supposedly built.

Another description that is believed to have come from the 4th century B.C. was related by Strabo, who wrote his famous work *Geography* around 20 B.C. Historians believe that Strabo relied on a history of Alexander the Great written by Onesicritus in the 4th century. Strabo relays the following comments:

> "Babylon, too, lies in a plain;...The garden is quadrangular, and each side is four plethra in length. It consists of arched vaults, which are situated one after another, on checkered cube-like foundations. The checkered foundations, which are hollowed out, are covered so deep with earth that they admit of the largest of trees, having been constructed of baked brick and asphalt—the foundations themselves and the vaults and the arches. The ascent of the uppermost terrace-roofs is made by a stairway; and alongside these stairs there were screws, through which the water was continually conducted up into the garden from the Euphrates by those appointed for this purpose, for the river, a stadium in width, flows through the middle of the city; and the garden is on the bank of the river." (*Geography*, XVI 1.5)

Like the previous description, this description also gives the impression of a mountain-like terrace. It also contains similar descriptions of the foundations of the garden and mentions the water-raising device. This time, Strabo specifically uses the term "screw" to describe the device. Both sources reference the river as the source of the water for the gardens.

The next source in this chronological order is Quintus Curtius Rufus, who wrote a history of Alexander the Great himself. He is also believed to have drawn on Cleitarchus of Alexandria, like Diodorus before him, as well as another 4th century writer named Ctesias. Rufus has the following comments to make about the Hanging Gardens,

> "On the summit of the citadel are the Hanging Gardens, a trite theme with the Greek poets; they equal in height the walls of the town, and their numerous lofty trees afford a grateful shade. The trees are twelve feet in circumference, and fifty feet in height: nor, in their native soil, could they be more productive. Supporting these are twenty dense walls, distant from each other twenty feet, surmounted with ranges of stone piers, over which is extended a quadrangle pavement of stone, strong enough to bear earth amassed high, and water supplied for irrigation. A distant spectator of these groves would suppose them to be woods nodding on

their mountains. Notwithstanding time destroys, by insensible corrosion, not only human works, but even nature herself; yet this pile, pressed with the roots, and loaded with the trunks of so gigantic a plantation, still remains entire. Tradition affirms, that a king of Assyria, reigning in Babylon, executed this work to gratify his queen, who, delighting in forest scenery, persuaded her husband to imitate the beauties of nature by a garden on this imperial scale." (*History of Alexander*, V 1.35)

In this account, there is once again an emphasis on the mountain-like nature of these gardens, and the first description's seemingly confusing reference to a Syrian king is here clarified as an Assyrian who ruled the city of Babylon.

The next source is the Jewish historian Josephus, who wrote in the 1st century A.D. He quotes Berossus, a native Babylonian source dating from the 3rd century BCE. It is this Berossus who provides Josephus with the information on the Hanging Gardens that Josephus incorporated into two of his works. In the context of describing the Babylonian king Nebuchadnezzar II and his accomplishments, Josephus wrote:

"At his palace he had knolls made of stone which he shaped like mountains and planted with all kinds of trees. Furthermore, he had a so-called pensile paradise planted because his wife, who came from Media, longed for such, which was custom in her homeland. (*Jewish Antiquities* X, 11)

...and, within this palace he erected lofty stone terraces, in which he closely reproduced mountain scenery, completing the resemblance by planting them with all manner of trees and constructing the so-called Hanging Garden; because his wife, having been brought up in Media, had a passion for mountain surroundings." (*Contra Apionem* I, 19)

An engraving on an eye stone of onyx with an inscription of Nebuchadnezzar II.

Here, for the first time, the unnamed queen and king are actually identified, and this progression is noteworthy, because it is typical of the growth of legends and should immediately make readers cautious about the reliability of this new information. Josephus also highlighted the mountain-like nature of these gardens.

The latest surviving ancient Greek source to mention the Hanging Gardens is Philo of Byzantium, the Paradoxographer. He lived in the 4th century A.D. and wrote a Greek treatise on the Seven Wonders of the World (Dalley and Oleson, 2003, 11 n. 29). Included in this treatise is a lengthy description of the Hanging Gardens. The most recent translation of this text is quoted below:

> "The so-called Hanging Gardens have plants above ground, and are cultivated in the air, with the roots of the trees above the (normal) tilled earth, forming a roof. Four stone columns are set beneath so that the entire space through the carved pillars is beneath the (artificial) ground. Palm trees lie in place on top of the pillars, alongside each other as (cross-)beams, leaving little space in between. This timber does not rot, unlike others; when it is soaked and put under pressure it swells up and nourishes the growth from roots, since it incorporates into its own interstices what is planted with it from outside. Much deep soil is piled on, and then broad-leaved and especially garden trees of many varieties are planted, and all kinds of flowering plants, everything, in short, that is most joyous and pleasurable to the onlooker. The place is cultivated as if it were (normal) tilled earth, and the growth of new shoots has to be pruned almost as much as on normal land. This (artificial) arable land is above the heads of those who stroll along through the pillars. When the uppermost surface is walked on, the earth on the roofing stays firm and undisturbed just like a (normal) place with deep soil. Aqueducts contain water running from higher places; partly they allow the flow to run straight downhill, and partly they force it up, running backwards, by means of a screw; through mechanical pressure they force it round and round the spiral of the machines. Being discharged into close-packed, large cisterns, altogether they irrigate the whole garden, inebriating the roots of the plants to their depths, and maintaining the wet arable land, so that it is just like an ever-green meadow, and the leaves of the trees, on the tender new growth, feed upon dew and have a wind-swept appearance. For the roots, suffering no thirst, sprout anew, benefitting from the moisture of the water that runs past, flowing at random, interweaving along the lower ground to the collecting point, and reliably protects the growing of trees that have become established. Exuberant and fit for a king is the ingenuity, and most of all, forced, because the cultivator's hard work is hanging over the heads of the spectators." (translation by Dalley, 2013, 40-41)

There are several new elements in this latest description. Like all of the Greek writers mentioned so far, Philo is not believed to have visited Babylon firsthand but likely collected his material from other literary sources. Most striking in this description is the sharp change in description of the gardens, from mountain-like to a description of plants directly above spectators' heads. This aspect of the description, which seems to be implied by the name "Hanging Gardens", is noticeably absent from each of the earlier descriptions, leading to questions over the actual name "Hanging Gardens" itself.

Chapter 3: The Translation of the Name "Hanging Gardens"

The term "Hanging Gardens" has been ubiquitous for nearly 2,000 years, but one of the problems that English speakers have in conceptualizing the Hanging Gardens comes from the name itself. The English word "hanging" evokes for most readers images either of a floating garden with suspended plants or at least ivy-type plants that themselves 'hang' below the roots that secure them. In *The Hanging Gardens of Nineveh*, Karen Foster lists three different possibilities for how these gardens might have been "hanging":

> "(1) trees and bushes grow on substantial structures, looming or hanging above the head of the viewer; (2) vines trail over the edges of rooftops, terraces, and pergolas, again looming or hanging above the head of the viewer; and (3) plants grow in a sunken area, such that the viewer looms or hangs over the garden, even as the plants appear to be suspended or hanging without visible means of support." (Foster, 2004, 209)

The Greek word, *kremastos*, is an adjective derived from the root verb *kremaō*. The verb and adjective are used to describe people "hanging" from the gallows and objects "hanging" from peoples' necks. But interestingly, the Septuagint translation of the Book of Ezekiel provides the closest parallel to this context. The prophet Ezekiel is painting a word picture in his oracle about the king of Judah being taken to Babylon, and the English translation of the Greek Septuagint at this point reads as follows:

> "Therefore, this is what the Lord says:
>
> And it is I who will take some
>
> from the select parts of the cedar;
>
> I will snip off something
>
> from the top of their heart.
>
> And it is I who will transplant

on a high mountain.

And I will hang (*kremasō*) him

in a mountain of Israel high in the air.

And I will transplant him,

and he shall produce a shoot and bear fruit

and become a large cedar." (Ezek. 17:22-23, Pietersma, 2007, 959)

In the Hebrew original, the verb at the end of verse 22, translated by the Greek translators as "transplant", is the same exact verb that they translated as "hang" at the beginning of verse 23. The Hebrew verb, *šātal*, is one of several Hebrew verbs meaning "to plant", but its meaning is very specific. It is not a native word in Hebrew but was borrowed from Akkadian during the Babylonian captivity. The verb only appears in the works of Jeremiah, Ezekiel and two late psalms. The noun, *šitlu*, refers to offshoots of vines and trees. The verb that was formed from this noun essentially means "to make an offshoot". In other words, it suggests planting or transplanting an offshoot of a tree or vine in a cultivated setting where it would not grow otherwise. When this passage is viewed in light of the adjective for the famous gardens at Babylon, a hitherto unrecognized technical meaning becomes evident. In addition to their standard verb for "transplant," the Greek translators used a technical term for planting a tree on a hilly terrace.

It is in light of the Ezekiel passage that the Greek phrase "hanging gardens" makes more sense, and there is no need to turn to the three possible interpretations of the usual sense of "hanging" outlined by Foster in order to understand the construction and nature of these gardens. The Greek phrase "hanging gardens" likely referred to artificially planted gardens that were set on a slope.

This coincides with all of the classical sources that survived antiquity. The relevant passages read as follows. According to Strabo, "It consists of arched vaults which are located on checkered cube-like foundations. The ascent of the uppermost terrace-roofs is made by a stairway…" Philo makes similar comments, "The hanging garden has plants cultivated above ground level, and the roots of the trees are embedded in an upper terrace rather than in the earth. The whole mass is supported on stone columns…" The longest passage in this regard comes from Diodorus Siculus: "…and since the approach to the garden sloped like a hillside and the several parts of the structure rose from one another tier on tier, the appearance of the whole resembled that of a theatre. When the ascending terraces had been built, there had been constructed beneath them galleries which carried the entire weight of the planted garden and rose little by little one above the other along the approach; and the uppermost gallery, which was fifty cubits high, bore the highest surface of the park, which was made level with the circuit wall of the battlements of the city."

In each case, the author emphasizes the sloping and hill-like nature of the artificial and man-made structures in which the plants and trees grew. It is this feature that the "hanging" likely described, and as such, the description of Philo of Byzantium is most likely an error. Given this context, Philo's description reads more like an unwarranted elaboration by a writer who had not visited the garden itself. Unfamiliar with the technical term and its use in agricultural contexts, Philo of Byzantium used the broader meaning of the Greek term to let his imagination run wild.

Chapter 4: The Legend of Semiramis and the Hanging Gardens

Before diving into the anomalies and inconsistencies regarding the Hanging Gardens, it is important to first establish what the legend was regarding the origins of the Hanging Gardens.

In Classical Antiquity, there were actually two competing legends explaining these origins. In the early 4th century B.C., a Greek physician and historian named Ctesias wrote a 23-book history of Assyria and Babylon after being employed at the royal Persian court. The work is so rife with extraordinary legends and unbelievable tales that historians generally dismiss most of what Ctesias had to say out of hand, unless there is some compelling reason to accept what he says based on corroboration from other sources. Unfortunately, this latter situation rarely arises.

Ctesias describes a great Assyrian queen named Semiramis who is a veiled personification of the Assyrian goddess Ishtar. Like Ishtar, she was a warlike princess who attracted many lovers, almost all of whom she treated with contempt and cruelty. According to Ctesias, Semiramis was married to a king named Ninus (the founder of Nineveh), and she becomes the source of most of the Babylonian architectural structures that remained until Ctesias' time. (Gilmore, 1887, 98) According to the legend, it is she who founds Babylonia and builds roads, bridges and canals throughout the region. She also conquers Egypt, Ethiopia and Media, and she is the one responsible for the Akkadian portion of the Behistun inscription of Darius I carved on the famous wall relief (Schmitt, 1993, 444).

The Behistun inscription

It is in this context that Semiramis is also credited with the construction of the Hanging Gardens. This material, credited to Ctesias, was only preserved in the writings of the 1st century B.C. writer Diodorus Siculus.

The second competing tradition was passed down by Josephus, the Jewish historian living in the Roman Empire during the 1st century A.D. He wrote a great deal about the Jewish scriptures in an attempt to make them accessible to the Roman mind, and a significant amount of material in the Hebrew Bible revolves around the Jewish exile and captivity in Babylon. As such, Josephus wrote about Babylon frequently.

Josephus had been trained in the Roman tradition of collecting multiple oral and written sources for his historical accounts, so he learned about and made use of a native Babylonian history that a Babylonian priest named Berossus had written four centuries earlier. That said, it is doubtful that he had direct access to this work; it seems more likely that Josephus relied on other historians who themselves had read Berossus' work and cited it.

Regardless, Josephus credits Berossus with the information that he relates about Nebuchadnezzar II (Nabouchodonosorous) and the Hangings Gardens. Nebuchadnezzar is said to have constructed stone terraces planted with multiple varieties of trees and the Hanging

Garden in an effort to reproduce the mountain scenery that his Median wife, Amytis, daughter of King Umakishtar, missed so dearly. The Medes were an ancient civilization of Iranian descent, and though native Babylonian sources make no mention of the names of the wives of Nebuchadnezzar II, it is known that he married a Median princess before he was even crowned king.

Another Greek author and contemporary of Josephus, Quintus Curtius Rufus, made similar remarks in his *History of Alexander*, but there is a curious difference in wording. According to Quintus Curtius Rufus, it was "an Assyrian king, reigning in Babylon" who built the Hanging Gardens. At first blush, this would also seem to line up perfectly with Nebuchadnezzar II. It was Nebuchadnezzar's father, Nabopolassar, who succeeded in making Babylon an independent state once again after overthrowing the Assyrian domination that had been a daily part of life in Babylon since it was sacked and raided by Sennacherib several generations prior. Nabopolassar was able to accomplish his goal because he was himself an Assyrian official posted in Babylon at the time. Thus, since Nebuchadnezzar II was Nabopolassar's son, he could have been described as an Assyrian ruling in Babylon.

Unfortunately, there are gaping holes in the historical and literary record that cast doubt upon both legends.

Chapter 5: Discrepancies, Anomalies and Contradictions

If Nebuchadnezzar II had the Hanging Gardens built at Babylon for his wife, as the legend goes, then these gardens should have constituted a prominent feature of the landscape of the city. Just as visitors and travelers commented on the other wonders when they visited those cities, one would expect effusive praise and detailed descriptions of these gardens whenever the topic of Babylon came up. After all, the authors who did mention the gardens described at length and in great detail both the beauty of the sight and its technical ingenuity.

However, multiple reliable authors exclude this expected feature from their descriptions of Babylon, its landscape, and environs. Herodotus described Babylon in great detail, and he mentions the walls of Babylon, its palaces, its temples, and the customs associated with these temples, but he didn't make a single mention of these famed gardens. The absence is so glaring that Stephanie Dalley, a scholar at Oxford University who has pioneered the recent research into the Hanging Gardens, entitled one of her recent articles, "Why Did Herodotus not Mention the Hanging Gardens of Babylon?" In this article, Dalley begins by affirming a fact that late 19th century scholars doubted, that Herodotus likely did visit Babylon and have firsthand knowledge of the city. She goes on to demonstrate that the Neo-Babylonian empire to which Nebuchadnezzar II belonged considered itself the continuation of the Neo-Assyrian empire by pointing to various attempts to maintain a sense of continuity between the two dynasties. After making these two important points, Dalley asks her original question again, "Why did Herodotus not mention the Hanging Gardens?"

Other well-known ancient historians are also silent on the matter. No mention of the Hanging Gardens appears in the *Cyropaedia* by Xenophon either. This work was a biography of sorts of Cyrus the Great, and Babylon figures prominently as one of the empires that Cyrus destroyed. Here again, the absence of any mention of the Hanging Gardens is glaring.

In addition to those two famous Greek writers, several renowned Roman historians fail to mention the existence of the gardens. In Plutarch's biography of Alexander the Great, there is nothing about the Hanging Gardens. Perhaps just as surprising is the description of Babylon in Pliny the Elder's *Natural History*, where he describes the walls of Babylon and the great temple of Jupiter Bel but makes no mention of the Hanging Gardens. The Hanging Gardens, as described in other classical sources, are exactly the type of topographic feature that Pliny set out to describe for readers, yet they do not even warrant a nod from him.

After taking the time to summarize all of the available classical descriptions of the Hanging Gardens, the scholar E. A. Wallis Budge found them to be so self-contradictory that he declared emphatically, "In my opinion a Garden of this size and kind never existed at Babylon" (Budge, 1920, 298). However, historians are quite used to their ancient sources being at odds with each other on various details; after all, if history were so straightforward, even fewer historians would be able to make a living sorting these questions out.

E. A. Wallis Budge

A consideration of the historical topography of the region creates another formidable problem in relation to the Hanging Gardens. One of the reasons why archaeologists have had a field day in Mesopotamia is that the land is so flat that the rivers do not remain in a fixed course for long.

They were continually diverted into new courses in antiquity by either natural phenomena, such as flooding in the wet season, or artificially engineered changes in direction. For this reason, ancient cities that were originally built along the course of the river became abandoned and desolate centuries later if the river had changed its course.

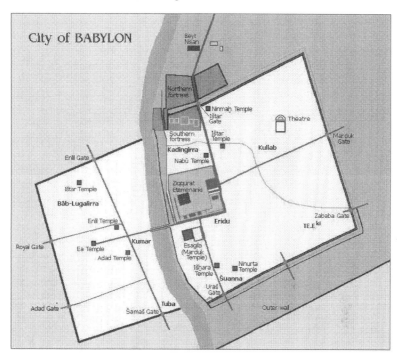

The layout of the city of Babylon in Nebuchadnezzar's time, with the palace complex in the middle.

In the case of Babylon, it was built along the Euphrates River and relied heavily upon the river for transportation of goods, which were sent on barges down the river, as well as its general water supply. The ancient descriptions of the Hanging Gardens indicate that its irrigation system was dependent upon the river, which obviously makes sense, but there are several historical problems based on the following facts. About a quarter of a century after the death of Nebuchadnezzar II, the Persians, led by Cyrus the Great, captured the city of Babylon in 539 B.C. As part of their military campaign to force Babylon to submit, the Persians diverted the Euphrates River away from the city, and it remained in its diverted course for centuries afterward, so that it no longer flowed through the palace complex (Dalley, 1994, 46). If the Persians diverted the river away from Babylon in the 6th century, how could 4th century sources like Ctesias and Berossus describe to their Greek audience a Babylonian garden watered by a river that was no longer there?

In the late 19th century, before archaeologists had excavated the vast caches of cuneiform tablets that can now be found in the British Museum, the Louvre and other famous museums throughout the world, the classical sources were the closest one came to the ancient Babylonian world. But now, a century and a half later, tens of thousands of these Babylonian cuneiform tablets have been deciphered and translated by scholars. Naturally, those translating the tablets figured that there would be a mention of such gardens by the Babylonians themselves, seeing as how they should have been a point of pride that would've inevitably peppered historical inscriptions and letters. Yet the Babylonian records remain silent on the matter of the Hanging Gardens. One text in particular, entitled the Topography of Babylon, would be the ideal place for the Babylonians to rave about their impressive Hanging Gardens, because this text takes up five cuneiform tablets and describes streets and temples and palaces of Babylon in great detail, yet the tablet says nothing about these famous gardens. Not only are the texts silent on the Hanging Gardens in particular; gardens and the act of gardening in general was not a subject that took any pride of place in the Babylonian texts available to us. Whereas the silence on the part of the classical sources is curious but not necessarily damning, the silence from native sources should give everyone pause.

The silence here is not only limited to the literary sources but extends to the archaeological record as well. Mesopotamia is one of the most professionally excavated regions in the world, and the city of Babylon, including the main palace complex, has been excavated extensively. Naturally, the first excavation team, led by Robert Koldewey, attempted to both identify and reconstruct the location of the Hanging Gardens within the palace complex. But ultimately, his identification and reconstruction were so faulty that just about every subsequent archaeologist and historian has torn it apart. The original excavation was unable to make a solid identification of the location of the Hanging Gardens, and no subsequent proposal for the location of the Hanging Gardens in Babylon has been able to garner any significant support.

Koldewey

All of this has ensured that the Hanging Gardens of Babylon are the most mysterious of all of the traditional Seven Wonders of the Ancient World. Given the unlikelihood that multiple ancient sources invented something out of thin air with alarmingly matching details, there was probably some magnificent garden in Mesopotamia connected with a queen that astonished the Greeks and the Romans. Yet the classical sources contain significant unexpected gaps in what they relate about the Hanging Gardens within other descriptions of the city of Babylon, and the topography of Babylon changed so significantly in terms of its water supply after the time of Nebuchadnezzar II that it could not have continued to support any such garden within the palace complex either. The Babylonian literature itself lacks any clear or even obscure or indirect reference to the Hanging Gardens, and the archaeology of the city of Babylon shows no trace of such a structural complex.

This led researchers to one inevitable question: where would the Hanging Gardens of Babylon have been located if not in Babylon?

Chapter 6: Does Babylon Actually Mean Babylon?

The gaps in the historical record, and the lack of evidence in the archaeological record, presented quite a conundrum for those looking for signs of the Hanging Gardens of Babylon, but eventually, work done in the late 20th century tried to make some sense out of the incomplete puzzle.

On the face of it, asking whether the "Babylon" in the Hanging Gardens of Babylon actually referred to the famous city itself is absurd. After all, Babylon was a well-known city in Mesopotamia and served as the capital of the Babylonian empire for most of its existence. On the other hand, the confusion evident both in the ancient sources and the modern archaeological record concerning the Hanging Gardens indicates that an innovative solution along these lines might just be warranted.

Eventually, Assyriologist Stephanie Dalley asked this bold question that previous scholars had not bothered to ask because it seemed nonsensical. She looked at the classical sources with an eye to whether they confused the city of Babylon or possibly conflated it with any other city, and she didn't have to look long before she found plenty of evidence to this effect. The first important source that she discovered in this connection was a series of astronomical observations from Azarqiel of Toledo written in Aramaic. This document makes reference to the longest day of the year from the perspective of "Old Babylon." In and of itself, this would not have been a very significant reference, except when it is combined with the identification of the latitude from which the observation must have been made. Based on the latitude calculations, the "Old Babylon" to which this document referred is not the ancient city of Babylon everyone thinks of today but actually the Assyrian city of Nineveh.

If there are ancient references to "Old Babylon," it begs the question as to the intended referent of its counterpart "New Babylon." Dalley painstakingly outlined how and when these names came into use within the native Akkadian sources themselves. When Assyrian leader Sennacherib sacked and destroyed Babylon in 689 B.C., his army smashed or removed all of the cult statues of the prominent gods within the city. This left the city godless, with no king and in a state of ruin for a quarter century or so, while its former inhabitants lived in exile. It was Sennacherib's son, Esarhaddon, who set to work rebuilding Babylon in an attempt to restore it to its former glory. The restored city that rose out of the ashes of the old was then appropriately dubbed the "New Babylon."

But this leaves the problem of when exactly Nineveh would have been referred to as Babylon. Although other kings adopted the title "king of Babylon" after they defeated the city, Sennacherib did not participate in this naming convention. Instead, for evidence that Nineveh was called Babylon, Dalley turns to the technical history of the textual tradition of one of the most prominent Akkadian myths: Enuma Elish, the Epic of Creation. In the traditional Old Babylonian version of this epic, Marduk defeats Tiamat and establishes Babylon as the center of the universe. In the Assyrian version of this Epic, the god Marduk, who was the traditional god of Babylon, has been replaced by Assur, the eponymous deity of the city of Assur and the Assyrians. What Dalley draws attention to is the fact that although the Assyrians took the time to change the name of the deity who forms the hero of the epic, they left the name of the city that he founded, Babylon, unchanged. For Dalley this makes little sense. If they were concerned about Assyrianizing the epic, why stop at the name of the deity and leave the Babylonian capital as the center of the world?

To answer the question, Dalley theorizes that the Assyrianizing process took place during the period of Sennacherib's reign, and that while the actual Babylon lay in ruins and was godless, the Assyrians began to call Nineveh by the name Babylon. After all, if Nineveh was referred to as Babylon, there would be no need for any further change to the text of the myth, because the renaming of Nineveh to Babylon would make it the center of the world. The god Assur, as the hero of the epic, now establishes Babylon as the center of the world, and Babylon now refers to Nineveh.

Of course, a trained historian is fully aware that a historical argument based on literary evidence such as this could not stand on its own without further support. To provide such support, Dalley garnered more evidence from several economic documents dated to Sennacherib's reign. The most important thing about these economic documents was the manner in which they were dated. Throughout the history of the two empires, the Assyrian and Babylonian, the two kingdoms used different dating systems. In the Babylonian empire, they used regnal years, such as the third year of King Nebuchadnezzar II's reign. In the Assyrian empire, they used what are called year eponyms, as in the year the king did something. In these economic documents, Dalley noted an interesting shift. Sennacherib's financial transactions were dated using the expected Assyrian system in the first half of his reign, but in the latter years of his reign, after he had sacked and destroyed Babylon, his scribes began using the Babylonian system of dating.

Evidence for the renaming of Nineveh as "Babylon" by the Assyrians appears in some of the surrounding cultures as well. The books of Chronicles in the Hebrew Bible present a retelling of the history of Israel and Judah, and at one point, they describe how the Assyrians took Manasseh captive to their capital city. But when the books name the capital city, they do not use the expected name Nineveh but instead use the name Babylon: "Therefore the LORD brought against them the commanders of the army of the king of Assyria, who took Manasseh captive in manacles, bound him with fetters, and brought him to Babylon" (2 Chr. 33:11). Not only was Babylon not the capital of Assyria, this was the very period when Babylon lay in ruins. As such, it is the exact period when Dalley argues that Nineveh was going by the name Babylon.

In addition to this Judean source, there is also a Greek source that provides evidence for the use of the name Babylon to refer to Nineveh. Diodorus Siculus describes many exploits of a legendary queen, whom he calls Semiramis, and she is identified as an Assyrian queen who is responsible for multiple building projects in "Babylon". At that time, however, the Assyrian rulers did not rule over Babylon, and just as importantly, the actual details of the building projects indicate that these projects were located in Assyria, most likely Nineveh, not Babylon. He wrote that Semiramis decorated her building projects with hunting scenes that included a wide variety of wild animals, and that the queen herself appears on one of these portraits riding horseback and impaling a leopard while her husband spears a lion beside her. As will be discussed further in detail below, this type of hunting and artistic imagery was unique to the Assyrians and did not appear in Babylon or as part of Babylonian art.

Diodorus Siculus' description, on its face, makes little sense, and classical scholars have long struggled to understand why Ctesias, Diodorus' native source, would have made such an elementary error. But in this new light, by recognizing that Nineveh for a time bore the name Babylon, and was referred to as "Old Babylon" when Babylon was rebuilt and became "New Babylon", the story makes perfect sense. An Assyrian queen was responsible for numerous building projects in Nineveh ("Old Babylon"), and the Assyrian style hunting scenes scattered throughout these building projects find a home in Nineveh that they would not have found in Babylon.

With all of this said, it must be acknowledged that in all of Dalley's work on this matter, she has failed to come up with any smoking gun that would remove any doubt as to the use of the name Babylon for Nineveh during Sennacherib's reign. But at the same time, the lack of such a smoking gun also might explain why no one came up with this solution to the problem presented by the Hanging Gardens sooner. The solution also has a great deal of explanatory power, since it reconciles the use of the term "Old Babylon" for Nineveh and helps explain several other historical oddities mentioned above.

Ultimately, the idea of Hanging Gardens themselves actually bolsters the argument that Nineveh was known as Babylon during the reign of Sennacherib, because one of the biggest differences between Nineveh and Babylon was the emphasis on gardening.

Chapter 7: A Regional Emphasis on Gardening and Gardens

Although both Nineveh and Babylon are both situated in what people immediately think of as the dry and arid climate of Mesopotamia, Babylon is located closer to the equator and thus experiences less annual rainfall than Nineveh. Climate maps show that Babylon is located in a region that receives only 100-200 mm of rainfall per year, whereas the city of Nineveh receives 600-1000 mm of rainfall annually. Babylon has a more desert-like climate, while Nineveh is more Mediterranean.

These distinct climate differences also expressed themselves in the distinctive cultures of each region. Understandably, both cultures prized water resources and fostered very adept engineers who mastered the art of controlling the flow of the rivers and developed innovative means for irrigating their fields, but in Babylon, the amount of water was so minimal that the focus of irrigation efforts was almost solely on crop production. The situation in Assyrian Nineveh was markedly different. Although water was still a valuable resource and one that needed to be protected and maximized, the Assyrians used water more freely than their Babylonian counterparts. The Assyrians not only raised crops but also grew ornamental gardens and parks whose purpose was more aesthetic than functional.

Assyrian kings also prided themselves on their hunting ability, which was a quite popular form of entertainment and sport in the royal court, and Assyrian kings built *ambassu*, which were large game parks where such sporting events could take place, and some of the most popular Assyrian reliefs that the general public is familiar with are those involving the king killing lions with a spear and similar weapons. This matches what is depicted in Ctesias' description of the wall that flanked the Hanging Gardens: "The height and width of this wall were even greater than those of the middle wall. On it, and on its towers, there were again wild beasts of every kind, cleverly drawn and realistically colored to represent a complete big-game hunt. These animals were more than 6 feet long, and Semiramis was portrayed among them, mounted and hurling a javelin at a leopard. By her side was her husband Ninus, dispatching a lion at close quarters with his spear." (Macqueen, 1964, p. 158). Such a description does not match any of the Babylonian motifs for art, but is a common theme in Assyrian art.

A bas relief from Sennacherib's palace depicts him during his war against Babylon

Furthermore, the Assyrians developed a strong literary tradition wherein the king would describe how he constructed various gardens in building inscriptions similar to those used for canals, palaces and temples. Not only was there such a strong literary tradition for gardens, but the Assyrian scribes used an interesting phrase in their descriptions of these gardens. They use the phrase *tamšil Ḥamāni* ("in the likeness of the Amanus mountains") to describe these gardens. This phrase highlights the fact that these gardens were not built in the style of the Western gardens of the time that favored symmetry with flowers and trees arranged in a central configuration (Oppenheim, 1965, 332); instead, they were constructed in the relatively flat plains of Assyria to model a hilly and wooded terrain with its winding footpaths and streams. The Assyrian monarchs not only conscripted literary descriptions of these gardens but adorned their palaces with bas reliefs depicting this lush terrain. Keeping these facts in mind, the presence of the Hanging Gardens in a place once called "Old Babylon" (Nineveh) would be entirely in keeping with what is known about the history and the values of the region and the culture. Conversely, trying to fit the Hanging Gardens into the traditional city of Babylon seems like trying to fit a square peg into a round hole.

Moreover, this new perspective helps to shed light on a comment found in Josephus's Babylonian source, Berossus, who talks about Nebuchadnezzar II building stone hills plated with all kinds of trees beside his Babylonian palace. This same Berossus provides one of the key Classical Greek descriptions of the Hanging Gardens. If Berossus had "Old Babylon" (Nineveh) in mind when he wrote about the stone hills and the Hanging Gardens, it would bring a great deal more credibility to the description and would easily explain how a non-native reader like Josephus could have mistaken Nineveh for the Babylon that stood at the center of the Babylonian empire.

Chapter 8: Native Descriptions of a Wonder?

In the 7th century B.C., the Assyrian king Sennacherib used the phrase "as a wonder for all people" ("*ana dagālu kiššat nišū*" in Akkadian) to describe his palace and accompanying gardens (VAB 4 138 ix 30). When dealing with two languages as different as Greek and Akkadian, it's important not to get too hung up on the fact that the same English word is used to translate both phrases from these two languages. What is more important in this context is that the Assyrian king, Sennacherib, thought his palace gardens were awe-inspiring for anyone who saw them, whereas the native Babylonian annals and documents make no such references to gardens and hardly make mention of gardening at all. This isn't that surprising given that the climate of Babylon did not lend itself to parks or gardens. Expending their precious few water resources on such extravagant pursuits as sport and aesthetic enjoyment would have ruined the economy by diverting necessary resources away from the production crops that supplied food for the city.

When Strabo described the Hanging Gardens and its irrigation system in great detail, he used the Greek term *kochlias* ("screw") to describe the mechanism that watered the gardens. This has proved to be another one of the many mysteries associated with the Hanging Gardens. Archimedes, who is generally credited with the invention of the screw as a water-raising device, did not invent this device until around 250 B.C., but it is clear that such a device was being used in Egypt in Ptolemaic times prior to Archimedes' version of the device (Stevenson, 1992, 48). The question is whether that engineering design could have already been in use in Mesopotamia three centuries before Ptolemy ruled Egypt. There was not a great deal of contact between the two civilizations before the 3rd century, and there is little reason to suspect that Greek engineers would have been allowed to study the technology involved in such an irrigation system. Moreover, because the mechanics of the system were internal, mere observation would not be sufficient to grasp and reproduce such technology.

That said, the ancient sources discussing the Hanging Gardens all make mention of some sort of engineering device that could raise water. For instance, Diodorus Siculous wrote, "…and there was one gallery which contained openings leading from the topmost surface and machines for supplying the gardens with water, the machines raising the water in great abundance from the river, although no one outside could see it being done." (Diodorus Siculus, Library 2.10). Unless the ancient accounts relating to the irrigation of the Hanging Gardens are all discounted, it is entirely possible that Mesopotamian agricultural engineers were years ahead of their time. In such an arid climate as Mesopotamia, irrigation technology was a key concern, so it makes sense that a great deal of time and finances were devoted.

Stephanie Dalley has taken this issue one step further. She found Assyrian texts that describe Sennacherib's palace and its associated gardens, and among these texts was a description of new technology for watering these gardens. In this text, Sennacherib uses a word for the hollowed out trunk of a palm tree, *alamittu*, to describe a screw that he used as a water-raising device. He explains how he cast the two separate components of this device using clay moulds, into which he then poured molten copper or bronze (Dalley, 1993, 8). The correspondence between this native Mesopotamian description and the description given by Strabo is striking to say the least. Here there is a Mesopotamian king boasting not only about the opulence and grandeur of his gardens but also the technology used to sustain it.

Scribes described the palace that Sennacherib built for himself as "The Palace without Rival" in multiple inscriptions. Two of these inscriptions were clay prisms, a popular shape of dedicatory inscriptions during the time, and another set were inscribed on a lion-sphinx. The extensive description of the garden associated with this palace appears on the prism inscriptions, and the detailed description of the irrigation system for these gardens appears on the lion-sphinx inscription without the accompanying description of the garden itself.

Perhaps most interesting of all is the dedication that appears on the lion-sphinx inscription immediately following the description of the Archimedean screw-type water-raising device. It reads:

> "And for Tašmētum-šarrat the queen, the chosen bride, my beloved, whose form Belet-ili has made more perfect than that of any other woman, I had a palace of loveliness, joy and happiness made, and so I put female lion-sphinxes of white limestone at its doors. At the command of Assur, father of the gods, and Ištar the queen, may we enjoy a long time together in those palaces in pleasure of the flesh and joy of the heart, may we have our fill of longevity. May a favourable *šedu* and a favourable *lamassu* always encircle the sides of those palaces forever, may their good omens never cease." (Dalley, 2002, 67-68)

Taken in the context of this proposal, Nineveh and Sennacherib would coincide with both traditional legends about the origin of the Hanging Gardens in a broad sense, since the gardens and the palace that they surround at Nineveh were dedicated to a queen. Furthermore, such a dedication of a building and its gardens to a queen is unique within the Assyrian and Babylonian traditions (Dalley, 2002, 68); one has to go to the Hittite or Luwian inscriptions to find anything comparable. This uniqueness only adds to the likelihood of identifying the Hanging Gardens with Sennacherib's garden structures at Nineveh, as opposed to anything built by Nebuchadnezzar II at Babylon.

Chapter 9: Problems with the Nineveh Theory?

Sometimes, in the process of attempting to solve a longstanding historical problem, the innovative solution creates new unforeseen problems once the implications of the new perspective are fully thought through. The situation with the Hanging Gardens is no different. There is no doubt that Dalley's theory that the Hanging Gardens were in Sennacherib's Nineveh, not Nebuchadnezzar II's Babylon, has many compelling points in its favor, but this reassessment of the historical material creates some new problems.

Without question, the most formidable problem relates to the history of Nineveh after Sennacherib, because seemingly all historical sources, including classical, Biblical and Babylonian sources, indicate that the great city of Nineveh met its fate at the hands of a coalition between Nebuchadnezzar II and the Medes in 612 B.C. In fulfillment of Assyrian curses and Biblical prophecies, the city was flooded and entirely destroyed. Thus, this raises a problem similar to the one regarding the diversion of the Euphrates River from Babylon. If Nineveh was ruined in the early 7th century B.C., it is impossible to understand how the magnificent Hanging Gardens were still standing from the 4th century B.C. through the 1st century A.D., when travelers were acclaiming it as one of the Seven Wonders of the World. Quintus Curtius Rufus makes the following comment about the Hanging Gardens as late as the 1st century A.D.: "Notwithstanding time destroys, by insensible erosion, not only human works, but even nature herself, yet this pile, pressed with roots, and loaded with the trunks of so gigantic a plantation, still remains entire."

The literary sources that relate the fall of Nineveh are quite varied in their ideological perspective, but they are in agreement on the major points. Chronologically, the first source is the Biblical prophet Nahum. He predicted the fall of Nineveh in an oracle only a few years before the event took place. The entire book of Nahum contains the superscription, "An oracle concerning Nineveh." Although the entire book of Nahum concerns the downfall of the city, the most relevant passages read as follows:

> "He calls his officers;
>
> They stumble as they come forward;
>
> they hasten to the wall,

and the mantelet is set up.

The river gates are opened,

the palace trembles.

It is decreed that the city will be exiled…" (Nahum 2:5-7)

"Nineveh is like a pool

whose waters run away." (Nahum 2:8)

"The crack of whip and rumble of wheel,

galloping horse and bounding chariot!

Horsemen charging,

flashing sword and glittering spear,

piles of dead,

heaps of corpses,

dead bodies without end—

they stumble over the bodies!..." (Nahum 3:2-3)

"Then all who see you will shrink from you and say,

'Nineveh is devastated; who will bemoan her?'

Where shall I seek comforters for you?" (Nahum 3:7)

"Yet she will become an exile,

she went into captivity;

even her infants were dashed in pieces

at the head of every street;

lots were cast for her nobles,

all her dignitaries were bound in fetters…" (Nahum 3:10)

"...fire has devoured the bars of your gates." (Nahum 3:13, NRSV)

As a forward looking prophecy, this information provides very little reliable information for the historian. Each of these things could have taken place, some of them could have taken place, or none of them could have taken place. The passage about the river gates being opened and Nineveh becoming a pool has been paired with the much later statement from the historian Diodorus Siculus, who states that Nineveh was destroyed in a three-year siege when the Euphrates flooded and breached the walls of the city. The problem with Diodorus' account is that the city of Nineveh does not lie on the Euphrates River but rather on the Tigris. Moreover, the features of the Tigris River would not have allowed it to flood the city as Diodorus described.

Van de Mieroop has studied this account of Diodorus and his source Ctesias and argues that it is not simply that Ctesias was an idiot and did not know what he was talking about. Rather, the Babylonians viewed their successful attack on Nineveh as payback for Sennacherib's attack on Babylon years earlier (van de Mieroop, 2004, 3). As such, the Babylonian literary accounts that described the attack on Nineveh described them as parallel events. In essence, the Babylonians were boasting that they did to Nineveh what Sennacherib had done to Babylon. The flooding of the river was something that happened to Babylon, not necessarily to Nineveh, but to keep the accounts consistent, both cities were said to have been flooded by the river. This style of parallel narratives also helps to explain why Ctesias would have written the wrong name of the river, and also why Ctesias describes a three-year siege of Nineveh, when this was a characteristic of the siege of Babylon, not of Nineveh. While the city was clearly destroyed in 612 B.C., it was not flooded as many historians used to suggest.

The Babylonian Chronicle is probably the most reliable historical account of the destruction of the city, but it is certainly not free of bias. The relevant portion reads as follows:

> "Twelfth year: When, in the month of Abu, the Medians...against Nineveh...they rushed and seized the town of Tarbisu, a town belonging to the province of Nineveh,...they went downstream on the embankment of the Tigris and pitched (camp) against Ashur. They made an attack against the town and [took the town], [the wall of] the town was torn down, a terrible defeat/massacre they inflicted upon the entire population. They took booty (and) carried pri[soners away]...

> [Fourteenth year]: The king of Akkad cal[led up] his army and [Cyaxar]es, the king of the Manda-hordes (Umman-manda) marched towards the king of Akkad, [in]...they met each other. The king of Akkad...and [Cyaxar]es...[the...]s he ferried across and they marched (upstream) on the embankment of the Tigris and...[pitched camp] against Nineveh...From the month Simanu till the month Abu, three ba[ttles were fought, then] they made a great attack against the city. In the month Abu, [the ...th day, the city was seized and a great defeat] he inflicted

[upon the] entire [population]. On that day Sinsharishkun, king of Assy[ria fled to]…, many prisoners of the city, beyond counting, they carried away. The city [they turned] into ruin-hills and hea[ps (of debris). The king] and the army of Assyria escaped (however)…" (Pritchard, 1969, 304-5)

Based on the Babylonian Chronicle, it is clear that the city was destroyed and its population decimated, but this begs the question of what happened to the gardens and their structures. Armies do not typically focus on destroying plants and vegetation, so while it is possible that they destroyed anything with an air of beauty about it, that would not necessarily be a foregone conclusion. Many of the measures that they might take to destroy the beauty of the gardens, like chopping down tree limbs or trampling flowerbeds, would be short-lived, and the effects would not last more than a few seasons.

In fact, the archaeological evidence indicates that the city of Nineveh continued to be occupied throughout the last few centuries B.C. and the first centuries A.D. (Stronach and Codella, 1997, 147). A building identified as the Hermes Temple was found in 1954 at the site, and the English translation of the Arabic excavation report reads:

> "In October 1954 the custodian of the Nineveh remains directed the attention of Mohammed Ali Mustafa to a piece of limestone he had discovered sticking out of the ground a little more than 100m north of the north-west corner of Nebi Yunis…The area surrounding the shrine was examined. It rose about 1m above the surrounding plain and extended for some distance, in the south running under the newly constructed houses. The high elevation suggests a Hellenistic settlement. This is supported by the discovery three years earlier of a limestone altar of Assyrian origin bearing a cuneiform inscription of Sennacherib on one side and a Greek inscription on the other. The altar was surrounded by pieces of stone and further investigation ascertained that the locality was the site of a large building whose foundations were of large blocks of limestone: perhaps the site of another Hellenistic temple… All these features, pointing towards the existence of a Hellenistic settlement in Nineveh, have been found on the west side of the city…" (Scott and MacGinnis, 1990, 69-70)

The difference in situation between that of the multiple problems for Babylon and the Hanging Gardens as compared with the new problems facing Nineveh and the Hanging Gardens is extraordinary. Whereas digging deeper into the historical evidence regarding Babylon and the Hanging Gardens continued to reveal more and more problems with such an identification, the more historical information researchers learn about Nineveh, the fewer problems exist for locating these famed gardens at Nineveh.

As the various accounts, historical facts, and theories make clear, the Hanging Gardens are by far the most mysterious of the ancient Seven Wonders of the World. Ironically, the ancient sources are fraught with difficulties and contradictions, but the biggest contradictions seemingly vanish when the Hanging Gardens of Babylon actually become the Hanging Gardens of Nineveh. While it might be impossible to ever determine the location of the ancient wonder with certainty, it was at the Assyrian capital that Sennacherib boasted that he constructed a garden to rival all gardens as a wonder for the entire world to see, replete with a description of the innovative water-raising device used centuries before Archimedes made his screw. He even dedicated his palace and the accompanying gardens to his queen and left inscriptions declaring his devotion to her.

If the Hanging Gardens were indeed Sennacherib's feat, it produces one of antiquity's greatest ironies. In Sennacherib's zeal to take all glory from Babylon by sacking the city, hauling off its deities and giving his capital city of Nineveh the name Babylon, he may have inadvertently given credit for one of his proudest accomplishments to his arch-nemesis.

Bibliography

Budge, E. A. Wallis. *By Nile and Tigris: A Narrative of Journeys in Egypt and Mesopotamia on behalf of the British Museum between the Years 1886 and 1913.* London 1920.

Clayton, Peter A. and Martin J. Price. *The Seven Wonders of the Ancient World.* London, 1988.

Dalley, Stephanie. "Ancient Mesopotamian Gardens and the Identification of the Hanging Gardens of Babylon Resolved." *Garden History* 21 (1993) 1-13.

Dalley, Stephanie. "Nineveh, Babylon and the Hanging Gardens: Cuneiform and Classical Sources Reconciled." *Iraq* 56 (1994) 45-58.

Dalley, Stephanie. "More about the Hanging Gardens." Pp. 67-73 in Lamia al-Gailani Werr, et. al. (eds.) *Of Pots and Pans: Papers on Archaeology and History of Mesopotamia and Syria Presented to David Oates in Honour of His 75ᵗʰ Birthday.* London, 2002.

Dalley, Stephanie. "Why Did Herodotus not Mention the Hanging Gardens of Babylon?" Pp. 171-89 in Peter Derow and Robert Parker eds. *Herodotus and His World:*

Essays from a Conference in Memory of George Forrest. New York, 2003.

Dalley, Stephanie. *The Mystery of the Hanging Garden of Babylon: an Elusive Wonder Traced*. Oxford, 2013.

Dalley, Stephanie and John Peter Oleson. "Sennacherib, Archimedes, and the Water Screw: The Context of Invention in the Ancient World." *Technology and Culture* 44 (2003) 1-26.

Foster, Karen. "The Hanging Gardens of Nineveh." (2004)

Gilmore, John. "The Sources of the Assyrian History of Ktesias." *The English Historical Review* 2 (1887) 97-100.

Macqueen, James G. *Babylon*. New York, 1964.

Oppenheim, A. Leo. "On Royal Gardens in Mesopotamia." *Journal of Near Eastern Studies* 24 (1965) 328-33.

Pietersma, Albert and Benjamin G. Wright (eds.). *A New English Translation of the Septuagint*. New York, 2007.

Schmitt, Rüdiger. "Ctesias." Vol. VI/4 pp. 441-46 in *Encyclopædia Iranica*. London, 1993.

Scott, M. Louise and John MacGinnis. "Notes on Nineveh." *Iraq* 52 (1990) 63-73.

Stronach, David and Kim Codella. "Nineveh." Vol. 4 pp. 144-48 in Eric M. Meyers (ed.) *The Oxford Encyclopedia of Archaeology in the Near East*. 5 Vols. New York, 1997.

van de Mieroop, Marc. "A Tale of Two Cities: Nineveh and Babylon." *Iraq* 66 (2004) 1-5.

Made in the USA
Coppell, TX
17 February 2025

46075879R00020